EVOLUTION

WHY DID FISH GROW FEET?

AND OTHER STORIES OF LIFE ON EARTH

By Anne Rooney

Contents

Once upon a Time...

Evolution is the story of life on Earth. It started with the tiniest living cells drifting through the oceans, and it's still going on today.

I'm Nippy and I'll be your expert tour guide for a fur-raising trip through time!

Living things have survived through freezing ice ages, blistering heat waves, devastating volcanic eruptions and deadly meteor strikes. They did it by changing and adapting. Animals and plants that adapt to suit changes around them live to tell the tale. The others die out. It's as simple as that.

Father of Evolution

The story of evolution starts with scientist Charles Darwin (1809-1882) – well, that's when the story of the story starts. On his travels in the Pacific Ocean he noticed that small birds called finches had differently shaped beaks on different islands. The beaks had changed to suit the foods available. Darwin realised that living things adapt!

Charles Darwin

Finches

Galapagos Islands

So if you want to know when fish grew legs, why the dinosaurs died out, or where humans fit into the story (pretty late!) read on… Ready to start the journey?

Let's go!

The Evolutionary Timeline

Along the bottom of each spread you'll see a strip of scientific-looking words. These are periods from Earth's history. **MYA** stands for "million years ago".

4,600 MYA EARTH FORMS

4600-542 MYA

PRECAMBRIAN

First living things

359-299 MYA

299-251 MYA

PERMIAN

CARBONIFEROUS

First reptiles

Dinosaur days

Dinosaurs ruled the Earth from around 230 to 65 million years ago. They ranged from truly gigantic (the largest animals ever to walk on land) to the size of a chicken.

251-200 MYA

TRIASSIC

First dinosaurs

200-145 MYA

145-66 MYA

JURASSIC

CRETACEOUS

Giant dinosaurs

Dinosaurs rule the Earth!

Evolution has been going on for a seriously long time. Experts reckon the first living things appeared a whopping **3,500 million years ago**. They were single cells that grew in rocks or underwater volcanoes, or maybe even arrived from space.

542-488 MYA

CAMBRIAN

488-444 MYA

ORDOVICIAN

444-416 MYA

416-359 MYA

SILURIAN

DEVONIAN

First amphibians

Fossils

A fossil is a record in rock of a plant or animal. There are many ways fossils form. Sometimes chemicals in the body are slowly replaced by rock. Sometimes a body or trace is encased by mud or ash that hardens and makes a cast.

Rodents like me popped up near the end of the Cretaceous.

Enter humans

Humans are recent arrivals. Modern people, known as *homo sapiens*, have only been around for about 200,000 years. That's just 0.004 per cent of the Earth's history!

66-23 MYA

23 MYA-NOW

NEOGENE

MASS DINOSAUR EXTINCTION

PALEOGENE

The start of grass

The age of humankind

Earth Gets Going

Our sun and its planets started as a whirling cloud of gas and dust 4,600 million years ago. Slowly, our own home, Earth, became a rocky world with vast oceans of water. And it's in the rocks and oceans that life first appeared, at least 3,500 million years ago.

The very first life forms were single **cells**, **microbes** so tiny that 5,000 could line up across your thumbnail. They lived in and fed on the rocks.

All that's left of those first microbes are the holes where they lived – fossilized holes!

Timeline!

PRECAMBRIAN 4600-542 MILLION YEARS AGO	CAMBRIAN 542-488 MYA	ORDOVICIAN 488-444 MYA	SILURIAN 444-416 MYA	DEVONIAN 416-359 MYA	CARBONIFEROUS 359-299 MYA

It was **cyanobacteria** that really set the ball rolling. These tiny organisms used sunlight to break down **carbon dioxide** and make the chemicals they needed to grow, just as plants do now. Food from sunlight still powers all living things in the world – plants make the food, and animals eat them (and each other).

Cyanobacteria

Each of the cyanobacteria made a hard shell. Together, they built rocky towers called **stromatolites.** The cyanobacteria made oxygen, and it started to escape from the sea into the **atmosphere.**

Disaster!

But everything alive was accustomed to low levels of oxygen and couldn't cope. Lots of the microbes died at the same time – the first **mass extinction.** The oxygen caused catastrophic climate change, too, triggering an ice age that lasted 300 million years.

Let's Get Together

At last, new organisms appeared that thrived on oxygen. They still only had a single cell, but these cells grew a **nucleus**. This meant organisms could store **genetic** information and pass on characteristics from one generation to the next.

About 1,200 million years ago, cells started to work together. Some held the group in place on the rock, and some focused on feeding. The cells adapted to their different jobs, and slowly the groups grew into the first organisms with multiple cells.

Bangiomorpha were some of the earliest multi-celled organisms. They had cells for reproducing (growing new bangiomorpha), and they **reproduced** sexually. That meant the new bangiomorpha had two parents, and inherited a mix of characteristics from them both.

Bangiomorpha

Modern algae is similar to early organisms like bangiomorpha.

PRECAMBRIAN
4600–542
MILLION YEARS AGO

CAMBRIAN
542–488 MYA

ORDOVICIAN
488–444 MYA

SILURIAN
444–416 MYA

DEVONIAN
416–359 MYA

CARBONIFEROUS
359–299 MYA

But it wasn't all sunny times by the seaside. About 950 million years ago, the world got much colder again. It was so cold it's been called Snowball Earth.

Some of the very first life forms were slimy algae. Yuck!

For millions of years, most of the Earth was frozen under a sheet of ice that stretched from the North Pole to the South Pole. Sometimes it would thaw and be hot for a million years or so. Then the weather would get cold again. It was a hard time for living things. But life adapts – that's what evolution is all about.

PERMIAN	TRIASSIC	JURASSIC	CRETACEOUS	PALEOGENE	NEOGENE
299–251 MYA	251–200 MYA	200–145 MYA	145–66 MYA	66–23 MYA	23 MYA–NOW

Life Explodes

At last, the world began to warm up and life got going again.

Life's as big as me, now!

Funisia was a pioneer. Rather than just making copies of itself, this upright, worm-like creature released eggs and **sperm** – female and male cells – into the sea. They combined and made a new Funisia with features of both parents. It was one of the first animals to do this.

Charnia's frondy, leaf-like body fed on chemicals or microbes in the water.

Charnia

Plant or animal?

Dickinsonia had a flat body up to a metre across and very thin. It probably absorbed food through its underside. It could have been a plant or an animal, or something in between.

| PRECAMBRIAN 4600–542 MILLION YEARS AGO | CAMBRIAN 542–488 MILLION YEARS AGO | ORDOVICIAN 488–444 MYA | SILURIAN 444–416 MYA | DEVONIAN 416–359 MYA | CARBONIFEROUS 359–299 MYA |

Then around 542 million years ago, something happened. Life really got going with a sudden eruption of new, different creatures. Most things still lived in the sea, but now it was a sea full of strange monsters. For the first time, some of the creatures had eyes. Before this time everything swam unseeing and unseen through the darkness.

Anomalocaris

fluttered through the sea on eleven pairs of flaps. It had a square mouth, surrounded by hard, square plates and sharp spikes, and was the largest Cambrian **predator**.

Opabinia

was small but freaky! It had five eyes – two pairs of two and a spare one in the middle. A long stalk or trunk on the front ended with spines for grabbing food, which it then passed to its mouth.

Hallucigenia

was a bizarre, prickly worm only 3 cm long. It crawled over rocks and the seabed on clawed legs.

Creepy Crawlies in the Sea

Trilobite

Modern Huntsman spider

Modern snail

Wiwaxia

Trilobites were part of a new group of animals called **arthropods**. Their bodies were divided into segments with hard outer shells. Later arthropods became crabs, shrimps, insects and spiders. Trilobites were so successful they survived for 270 million years.

The first **molluscs** were tiny sea snails and shellfish. They fed on plankton – microscopic plants and animals that drift freely in the sea. **Aldanella** looks like a snail, but **Wiwaxia** looks unlike any modern mollusc. It had a well-protected top surface with hard plates and sharp spikes. It moved over the sea bed scraping up algae with its underside.

| PRECAMBRIAN 4600-542 MYA | CAMBRIAN 542-488 MILLION YEARS AGO | ORDOVICIAN 488-444 MYA | SILURIAN 444-416 MYA | DEVONIAN 416-359 MYA | CARBONIFEROUS 359-299 MYA |

Some of these weird and wonderful creatures were doomed to die out leaving no trace, but others would stick around, in one form or another. The ancestors of insects, worms, molluscs and jellyfish all appeared in the Cambrian sea.

Plectronoceras looked like a squid with a shell and was the earliest cephalopod, a group which would include squid and octopus.

Modern earthworm

Worms first turned up in the sea, too. **Ottoia** was a curved worm up to 8 cm long that lived on the seabed, perhaps lurking in a burrow. It had a long trunk or **proboscis** with hooks on the end for grabbing food.

Ottoia

Haikouichthys was a very early type of fish. It had no jaws, but it did have gills and the earliest type of backbone, making it one of the first **vertebrates**.

Slow and slimy - not my favourite look.

PERMIAN 299-251 MYA	TRIASSIC 251-200 MYA	JURASSIC 200-145 MYA	CRETACEOUS 145-66 MYA	PALEOGENE 66-23 MYA	NEOGENE 23 MYA-NOW

Moving Inland

From the time when the first algae slimed the rocks at the water's edge, more and more life moved onto land. First, around 450 million years ago, tiny **arthropods** that looked a bit like spiders or millipedes crawled over the algae and the moss that developed from algae. But nothing ventured inland – there was no food there.

Fossil showing Devonian arthropods

Cooksonia

| PRECAMBRIAN 4600-542 MYA | CAMBRIAN 542-488 MYA | ORDOVICIAN 488-444 MYA | SILURIAN 444-416 MILLION YEARS AGO | DEVONIAN 416-359 MILLION YEARS AGO | CARBONIFEROUS 359-299 MYA |

Over millions of years, the algae adapted into early plants which drew water from the soil, meaning they could grow further from the sea. Seeds blown on the wind helped them spread further.

Weird...

Prototaxites was a sort of giant fungus-like plant that grew to 8 m tall and 1 m across.

Sigillaria

Archaeopteris

Lepidodendron

At first, most plants looked like **Cooksonia** (sce left), with spores growing at the tops of simple branches. But then plants got into their stride, and grew in all shapes and sizes. They developed strong stems to carry water and nutrients and support their own weight. By 370 million years ago, vast forests of early trees called **Archaeopteris** covered the land, and the ground crawled with spiders, centipedes, mites and early scorpions.

Plenty to eat! But not many creatures to eat it yet.

Plenty More Fish in the Sea

Back in the water, between 420-380 million years ago, fish ruled. In the race for food, some developed proper jaws, and many grew armoured plates over their heads or even their whole bodies. A few started to grow their babies inside them instead of making eggs that mixed with **sperm** in the water. This gave the babies a better chance of survival.

The fearsome **Dunkleosteus** was one of the largest creatures of its time. At 6 m long, with armoured plates on its head and neck, and with one of the most powerful bites ever known on Earth, it was pretty scary, especially if you looked like dinner.

| PRECAMBRIAN 4600-542 MYA | CAMBRIAN 542-488 MYA | ORDOVICIAN 488-444 MYA | SILURIAN 444-416 MYA | DEVONIAN 416-359 MILLION YEARS AGO | CARBONIFEROUS 359-299 MYA |

Stethacanthus

was an early shark with a bony blob on top of its head covered in tiny, tooth-like granules called denticles. There was another patch of shark-Velcro on top of its nose. No one knows what they were used for (although Stethacanthus probably did).

Paddle-shaped **Drepanaspis** skulked on the seabed. As a baby it was soft, but as it grew older, bony plates spread over its head. It had no fins besides its tail, and its mouth was on top – not a good design if it ate things that fell to the bottom.

I nip; these guys chomp!

| PERMIAN 299-251 MYA | TRIASSIC 251-200 MYA | JURASSIC 200-145 MYA | CRETACEOUS 145-66 MYA | PALEOGENE 66-23 MYA | NEOGENE 23MYA-NOW |

21

Legs for Land

And nearly 400 million years ago, some fish even grew legs!

Fishes with fingers!

From Fins to Legs

On the way to living on land, fish changed their **swim bladders** – which helped them to float – for lungs that could use air. Their skulls separated from their shoulders, allowing them to move their heads separately. Some of their fins grew longer and stronger so that they could splatter around in the mud at the edges of rivers and estuaries. They were the first **tetrapods** – animals with four legs.

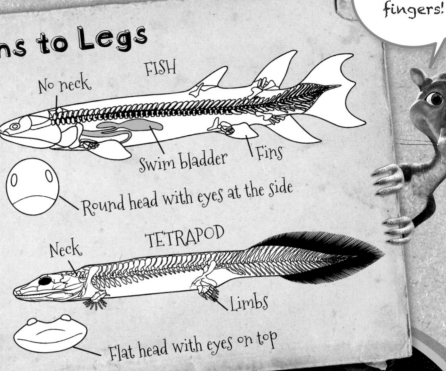

FISH

No neck

Swim bladder

Fins

Round head with eyes at the side

TETRAPOD

Neck

Limbs

Flat head with eyes on top

Osteolepis was still a fish, but might have used its lobe-shaped fins as flippers to push it over the mud on the riverbed.

Osteolepis

Acanthostega

Acanthostega probably paddled through shallow, muddy pools or rivers. Its ribs wouldn't support its weight on land, but it could lift its head to breathe air and snap up food. It might have used its weak legs to hold onto or push through plants.

22

PRECAMBRIAN
4600-542 MYA

CAMBRIAN
542-488 MYA

ORDOVICIAN
488-444 MYA

SILURIAN
444-416 MYA

DEVONIAN
416-359
MILLION YEARS AGO

CARBONIFEROUS
359-299 MYA

Ichthyostega lived on land and in the water. Its strong shoulders and front legs were good for dragging itself over the ground, while its back legs were better used as paddles in the water.

The early tetrapods might have been sluggish and blobby, but they would evolve to rule the world, first as dinosaurs and then as mammals, including us!

PERMIAN 299-251 MYA	TRIASSIC 251-200 MYA	JURASSIC 200-145 MYA	CRETACEOUS 145-66 MYA	PALEOGENE 66-23 MYA	NEOGENE 23MYA-NOW

23

Getting the Hang of It

The lumbering tetrapods that started as fish-out-of-water slowly adjusted to life on land.

Amphibians have babies that go through a stage as something else and then change – frogs start as tadpoles.

Some became **amphibians**, spending time on land and in the water. They went back to the water to produce young, but the adults spent time on land, breathing air.

Other tetrapods moved onto land completely and reproduced there. The female laid a shell-covered egg that could survive on land without drying out. These egg-laying tetrapods became **reptiles**.

Eryops looked a bit like a crocodile, but was an amphibian. Its short ribs did not go all the way under its chest to allow it to walk far on land. It lived in rivers and swamps.

24

| PRECAMBRIAN 4600-542 MYA | CAMBRIAN 542-488 MYA | ORDOVICIAN 488-444 MYA | SILURIAN 444-416 MYA | DEVONIAN 416-359 MYA | CARBONIFEROUS 359-299 MYA MILLION YEARS AGO |

Proterogyrinus

was one of the first animals to have strong enough ribs and chest muscles to support its weight while walking and breathing air on land. Called a reptilomorph, it was an amphibian that was on the way to being a reptile.

Proterogyrinus

While the amphibians stayed in the swamps and near water, the reptiles explored further afield, living in the forests and eating arthropods – and each other!

Hylonomus

was the earliest known reptile. Only about 20 cm long, it ate early insects and arthropods such as millipedes. It looked like a modern lizard, with legs that splayed out at the sides.

| PERMIAN 299-251 MYA | TRIASSIC 251-200 MYA | JURASSIC 200-145 MYA | CRETACEOUS 145-66 MYA | PALEOGENE 66-23 MYA | NEOGENE 23MYA-NOW |

25

Creepy Crawlies on Land

As the plants moved further inland, so did the animals. They changed over millions of years, becoming adapted to new living spaces. Some arthropods developed into insects, and some of those grew wings. They took to the air, becoming the very first creatures ever to fly over the Earth.

Meganeura

was a huge dragonfly, with wings up to 65 cm across. It dipped and dived over swamps in the prehistoric forest looking for creatures to eat. Giant mayflies grew to 45 cm across, while **Euphoberia** was a millipede a metre long.

PRECAMBRIAN 4600-542 MYA	CAMBRIAN 542-488 MYA	ORDOVICIAN 488-444 MYA	SILURIAN 444-416 MYA	DEVONIAN 416-359 MYA	CARBONIFEROUS 359-299 MYA MILLION YEARS AGO

The plants poured more and more oxygen into the air, changing the atmosphere. The oxygen was good for the arthropods and they thrived, growing enormous.

To think those arthropods began by eating mud. They've come a long way.

But that wasn't the biggest. By 340 million years ago, **Arthropleura** clattered over the forest floor, growing up to 2.4m long – as long as an alligator! Although it looks scary, it ate only plants. Nothing was big enough to hunt it, and it only died out when the climate changed and the forests it lived in turned to desert.

A Bit Mammalian

To start with, the synapsids were squat and stocky, with splayed, wide-set legs. Some had wide, barrel-shaped chests with space for a large gut to digest the tough plant material they ate. Others were carnivores, adapted to hunting.

Ophiacodon

had splayed legs and toes, and a long snout packed with 166 sharp teeth. It lurked in the water, eating fish and lying in wait for other, smaller, tetrapods. It was a synapsid, and crocodiles are reptiles, so although ophiacodon looked similar, it's not related.

PRECAMBRIAN 4600-542 MYA	CAMBRIAN 542-488 MYA	ORDOVICIAN 488-444 MYA	SILURIAN 444-416 MYA	DEVONIAN 416-359 MYA	CARBONIFEROUS 359-299 MILLION YEARS AGO

You wouldn't catch me lying in the sun. I'm warm-blooded!

You can easily spot **Dimetrodon** by the huge sail on its back, supported by bones growing from the spine. Its large area helped dimetrodon warm up in the sun. All animals were still **cold-blooded** at this time, meaning they couldn't control their body temperature alone and needed the sun's warmth.

Cotylorhynchus was the largest of all synapsids. Up to 6 m long and weighing 2 tonnes, it was big enough to scare off even a hungry dimetrodon. It ate a lot of plants, but they were not very **nutritious**, so it probably spent all day eating to get enough nutrients.

PERMIAN 299-251 MILLION YEARS AGO	TRIASSIC 251-200 MYA	JURASSIC 200-145 MYA	CRETACEOUS 145-66 MYA	PALEOGENE 66-23 MYA	NEOGENE 23MYA-NOW

29

Fighting and Fighting Back

Scutosaurus

was a reptile, not a synapsid, but went along with the fashion for sabre-teeth or tusks. This stocky herbivore had bony plates called "scutes" all over its back – and two tusks that hung down beneath its mouth. It might have used them to defend itself or to grub out roots.

As time passed, the synapsids became more specialized. The **carnivores** grew longer legs, becoming faster, more agile hunters. Their teeth became well suited to hunting, with sharp front teeth for holding and tearing at prey and wide back ones for chewing and crunching.

PRECAMBRIAN	CAMBRIAN	ORDOVICIAN	SILURIAN	DEVONIAN	CARBONIFEROUS
4600-542 MYA	542-488 MYA	488-444 MYA	444-416 MYA	416-359 MYA	359-299 MYA

Robertia

Robertia looked something like a slim, bald guinea pig with sabre-teeth. It ate plants, and might have used its tusks for digging up roots. A notch in the top of its mouth was handy for holding tough plant stems in place while its horny beak snipped through the stalks.

Moschops

was a huge, heavy, plant-eater that might have grazed in herds, munching leaves and branches. It may have used its thick, bony skull in head-butting contests, perhaps to fight over mates. Or the skull could have been for fighting with predators.

Titanosuchus,

looked like a crocodile, but was really a synapsid. At more than 2.5 m long and with large fang-like teeth, it could easily kill and eat a Moschops.

Sabre-toothed synapsids like

Inostrancevia

were well-suited to life as hunters. Inostrancevia was huge - about the size of a modern rhinoceros. It used its giant teeth for ripping apart its prey.

My teeth are the same design! But smaller.

Everything seemed to be going along nicely, with synapsids and reptiles sharing the world, and the amphibians taking a back seat. But then –

disaster!

Around 252 million years ago, something bad happened. It may have been a huge volcano pouring out scorching lava, poisonous fumes and sky-darkening ash. Or perhaps a giant meteor hit Earth. Either would bring first freezing darkness, then searing heat, and acid rain, devastating both land and sea.

The terrible event wiped out 95 per cent of all species. Vast forests and the animals living there vanished. Many insects disappeared, followed by the reptiles that ate them. Fish died, and the fish-eating amphibians. A world that had been teeming with life became barren.

Eventually, the climate settled. There were just a few hardy survivors like...

Lystrosaurus

was a stocky plant-eating synapsid with tusks. Lystrosaurus quickly spread all over the world because it was adaptable: it ate whatever plants it found.

32

PRECAMBRIAN	CAMBRIAN	ORDOVICIAN	SILURIAN	DEVONIAN	CARBONIFEROUS
4600-542 MYA	542-488 MYA	488-444 MYA	444-416 MYA	416-359 MYA	359-299 MYA

Thrinaxadon was a meat-eating synapsid that looked more like a mammal than Lystrosaurus did, with legs coming out directly under the body, not out at the sides.

Euparkeria appeared soon after the extinction. An early archosaur, it had long legs for speed, lots of sharp teeth, a good sense of smell and sharp claws.

Land for Lizards

Within 5 million years the survivors had evolved to fill the gaps left by those that died out. And who came to rule the land? The archosaurs. Their name even means "ruling lizards".

You know what comes after archosaurs, don't you? Some more famous "saurs".

PERMIAN 299-251 MILLION YEARS AGO	TRIASSIC 251-200 MILLION YEARS AGO	JURASSIC 200-145 MYA	CRETACEOUS 145-66 MYA	PALEOGENE 66-23 MYA	NEOGENE 23MYA-NOW

From Archosaur to Dinosaur

As the world settled down, the archosaurs emerged as top dogs. They split into two main groups. Some had ankles with hinged joints, which meant they could run fast – they developed into dinosaurs and pterosaurs. Others had ankles with rotating joints, like a ball held in a cup – they developed into crocodile-like reptiles.

Archosaurs still exist! Crocodiles and birds are both types of archosaur.

Joint Types

HINGED

ROTATING

Joint hinges like a human elbow

Joint rotates like a human shoulder

Eoraptor, which lived 231 million years ago, was one of the earliest dinosaurs – perhaps the earliest of all. It was probably an **omnivore**, eating anything it could find.

| PRECAMBRIAN 4600–542 MYA | CAMBRIAN 542–488 MYA | ORDOVICIAN 488–444 MYA | SILURIAN 444–416 MYA | DEVONIAN 416–359 MYA | CARBONIFEROUS 359–299 MYA |

Herrerasaurus already had features that became common in later dinosaurs. It was a **theropod**, a group that would include fierce, fast meat-eaters like *T. rex*, Its powerful back legs, short front legs and strong jaws filled with blade-like teeth show that Herrerasaurus chased and ate other animals.

Riojasaurus was a sauropodomorph. This type of dinosaur would later develop into giant **sauropods** like diplodocus. A plant-eater up to 5 m long, Riojasaurus walked on four legs and couldn't run fast if attacked.

Postosuchus looks a bit like *T. rex*, but wasn't a dinosaur. It was a crocodile-like archosaur. They look similar because both adapted to live in much the same way – chasing and eating other large animals.

Nearly the Same, but Different

Just as Postosuchus looked a bit like *T. rex*, some other Triassic animals looked alike but were not related. When animals evolve the same features even though they are not related, it's called **convergent evolution**.

Effigia
was an archosaur, but like many dinosaurs its beak was suited to snapping through tough plants or cracking seedpods, and its powerful leg muscles were adapted to run fast.

Coelophysis
looked rather similar to Effigia but was a carnivore. One of the earliest dinosaurs, it was very successful. It might have hunted in packs, or just jumped on prey all by itself.

| PRECAMBRIAN 4600–542 MYA | CAMBRIAN 542–488 MYA | ORDOVICIAN 488–444 MYA | SILURIAN 444–416 MYA | DEVONIAN 416–359 MYA | CARBONIFEROUS 359–299 MYA |

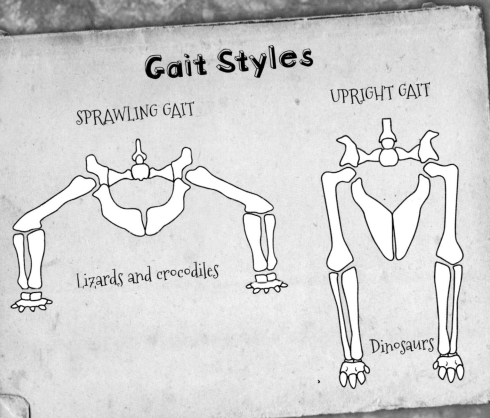

Gait Styles

SPRAWLING GAIT

UPRIGHT GAIT

Lizards and crocodiles

Dinosaurs

Dinosaurs could run more quickly than reptiles shaped like lizards because of how their hips worked. Lizards and crocodiles both have a sprawling **gait**, meaning their legs stick out to the sides of their bodies. Dinosaurs had legs that grew underneath their bodies in an upright gait.

My legs come out underneath my body, and so do yours!

Eocursor was a type of dinosaur called an **ornithischian**. Like Effigia, it had a beak, a long neck and tail, long, strong rear legs and shorter front legs. Dinosaurs with horny beaks would later evolve into very different shapes.

Take to the Skies!

While the dinosaurs and the crocodile-like archosaurs were trundling or scurrying around on the ground, another type of archosaur was taking to the air. Pterosaurs were flying reptiles, and the first creatures other than insects ever to fly.

Unlike birds, many pterosaurs had teeth rather than beaks, and bones running right to the ends of their whip-like tails. Pterosaurs were very successful, surviving for 170 million years.

Modern birds all have short tails. The extra length you see is just feathers.

The earliest pterosaur, **Eudimorphodon**, was quite small, weighing just 10 kg. It had a mix of fangs and sharp, pointed teeth that were good for catching and grasping fish.

PRECAMBRIAN 4600–542 MYA	CAMBRIAN 542–488 MYA	ORDOVICIAN 488–444 MYA	SILURIAN 444–416 MYA	DEVONIAN 416–359 MYA	CARBONIFEROUS 359–299 MYA

The smallest pterosaurs were a few centimetres long – just the size of a sparrow. But the biggest, and one of the last, was a giant. **Quetzalcoatlus** was the size of a small plane, at 12 m across. It's the largest animal ever to have flown.

Pterodactyls

soared through the Jurassic sky. They measured up to 1.5 m across, with a short tail.

Pteranodons were a late type of pterosaur with a toothless beak, a bony crest and a short tail that ended in a rod of fused bones.

Back to the Water

It's all very well getting a taste for breathing air, but there was a lot more water than dry land. The reptiles weren't about to give up world **domination** by leaving the water to the fish. So back they went…

Mixosaurus is the earliest known ichthyosaur, or "fish lizard". Its legs reverted to stumpy flipper-shapes, and its body became streamlined. It had the body-plan of a fish without actually being a fish, because that's the best shape to be if you need to move quickly through water.

Modern dolphins also look like fish, but they're mammals like me and you. Convergent evolution again!

PRECAMBRIAN	CAMBRIAN	ORDOVICIAN	SILURIAN	DEVONIAN	CARBONIFEROUS
4600-542 MYA	542-488 MYA	488-444 MYA	444-416 MYA	416-359 MYA	359-299 MYA

It wasn't just the reptiles that reclaimed their watery heritage. **Mastodonsaurus** was the largest amphibian ever to live. At 6 m long, it looked like a large, thickset crocodile with no neck. Its eyes were on top of its head, making it easy for it to see above the surface of the water without revealing itself.

Nothosaurus

was a long, slender sea-going reptile that also spent time lounging about on rocks. With teeth adapted to eating fish and legs like flippers, it lived rather like a seal does today.

Henodus looks like a modern turtle, which is also a reptile. It was hardly streamlined, but its hard shell protected it from predators. It lived at the bottom of the sea, eating shellfish with its two teeth and hard beak.

| PERMIAN 299-251 MYA | TRIASSIC 251-200 MILLION YEARS AGO | JURASSIC 200-145 MYA | CRETACEOUS 145-66 MYA | PALEOGENE 66-23 MYA | NEOGENE 23 MYA-NOW |

All Change!

No sooner had everything settled down when it all went wrong again. 201 million years ago, after just 50 million years of calm, catastrophic climate change killed at least three quarters of all species on Earth. Again.

The Changing World

At the same time as the extinction, and probably related to it, **Pangaea** (a giant landmass) started to break apart. Over 620,000 years, volcanoes tore the land apart. North and South America separated, and only a small land-bridge connected Africa to the rest of the landmass. Slowly, the brand new Atlantic Ocean began to fill the gap between Africa and the Americas.

When all the land was joined together, animals and plants could spread without limits. But when vast oceans separated the continents, plants and animals couldn't cross them. They started to develop separately.

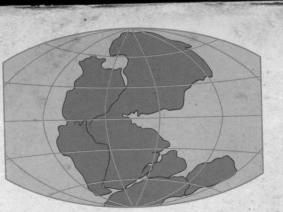

Permian 251 million years ago

Jurassic 145 million years ago

Present day

42

| PRECAMBRIAN 4600-542 MYA | CAMBRIAN 542-488 MYA | ORDOVICIAN 488-444 MYA | SILURIAN 444-416 MYA | DEVONIAN 416-359 MYA | CARBONIFEROUS 359-299 MYA |

Most large amphibians and many other reptiles died out, as did quite a few dinosaurs. That left the coast clear for the remaining dinosaurs and other reptiles to take over.

This was a really quick extinction – but it still took about 10,000 years.

Sarcosaurus

was a carnivorous dinosaur about 3 m long. It survived the end-Triassic extinction event.

The herbivore

Scelidosaurus

also survived. It would have been a struggle for Sarcosaurus to snack on Scelidosaurus, which was 4 m long and quite spiky.

| PERMIAN 299-251 MYA | TRIASSIC 251-200 MILLION YEARS AGO | JURASSIC 200-145 MILLION YEARS AGO | CRETACEOUS 145-66 MYA | PALEOGENE 66-23 MYA | NEOGENE 23 MYA-NOW |

Jurassic Giants

Dinosaurs grew and grew
and grew until they were giants.
The largest of all were the **Sauropods** –
huge, plant-eating dinosaurs that became the
largest animals ever to walk on Earth.

Sauropods could reach the treetops and eat food that no one
else was eating. But tough plant matter isn't very nutritious,
so they needed to eat a lot. That meant they needed big
bellies, and then they needed big, thick legs to support
their big bellies, so they got
bigger and bigger.

| PRECAMBRIAN 4600–542 MYA | CAMBRIAN 542–488 MYA | ORDOVICIAN 488–444 MYA | SILURIAN 444–416 MYA | DEVONIAN 416–359 MYA | CARBONIFEROUS 359–299 MYA |

Amphicoelias

was the biggest of the big. At up to 60 m long, it was nearly twice the length of a blue whale, making it the largest animal ever.

One toe could crush me! I have to nip out of their way!

Diplodocus was smaller

– only half the size at just 26 m. Like other giant sauropods, it probably held its head and tail in a straight, horizontal line except when it wanted to stretch its head up or down.

Tail flick trick!

By flicking the ends of their tails like a whip, giant sauropods could make a sonic boom as the end of the tail broke the sound barrier! It would have sounded like a cannon firing.

Apatosaurus was another

giant sauropod. Like the others, it walked on all fours, though the young could rear up and run on two legs.

Running Scared

Those huge sauropods must have looked like a mega-dinner to the meat-eaters of the Jurassic world – but they were just too big to tackle.

> I'm glad there's a few million years between these guys and me!

Meat-eaters need to be nimble enough to chase prey, and big animals are not generally very fast. The biggest therapod dinosaurs were much smaller than the monster sauropods. The smaller – but still pretty big – plant-eating **ornithopods** were just the right size for a hungry carnivore, so they had to run fast if they were to get away.

Allosaurus ran fast on two strong back legs, its heavy head was balanced by a thick tail, and it used its short arms with super-strong claws to clutch and tear its prey. Teeth 10 cm long pointed backwards, so prey couldn't wriggle out of its bite.

PRECAMBRIAN	CAMBRIAN	ORDOVICIAN	SILURIAN	DEVONIAN	CARBONIFEROUS
4600–542 MYA	542–488 MYA	488–444 MYA	444–416 MYA	416–359 MYA	359–299 MYA

At 10-12 m long, **Saurophaganax** could take on quite a big sauropod. An Apatosaurus was fair game, at only twice Saurophaganax's length – especially as a lot of the length of an Apatosaurus is its neck and tail. Saurophaganax might have been a type of big Allosaurus.

Camptosaurus only ate plants, and was small enough that an Allosaurus stood a chance of tackling it – but it could run away at 25 kph. Its triangular-shaped head had a hard beak for snipping off leaves and branches.

PERMIAN
299-251 MYA

TRIASSIC
251-200 MYA

JURASSIC
200-145
MILLION YEARS AGO

CRETACEOUS
145-66 MYA

PALEOGENE
66-23 MYA

NEOGENE
23 MYA-NOW

47

Plates, Spikes, Sails and Scales

An Allosaurus might think it would be easy to grab a **Stegosaurus** by the neck. But look out for the tail! Stegosaurs of all types had a scary, spiky tail weapon, sometimes called a thagomizer. Stegosaurus could swipe it round to the side, thwacking a meat-eater hard. Some Allosaurus bones have been found with partly healed injuries that match Stegosaurus thagomizer spikes.

Hot plates

The plates on the stegosaur's back were probably used for display or to help control its body temperature. For display, they might have been able to change colour to attract a mate or scare a predator. To regulate heat, they might have absorbed heat from the sun, or let the wind cool blood flowing through the plates.

PRECAMBRIAN	CAMBRIAN	ORDOVICIAN	SILURIAN	DEVONIAN	CARBONIFEROUS
4600-542 MYA	542-488 MYA	488-444 MYA	444-416 MYA	416-359 MYA	359-299 MYA

Not all plant-eaters relied on speed to get away from hungry carnivores. Some were slow and stocky, but had other defence strategies. If you can't run away, you need either to fight back or to be difficult to eat.

Gargoyleosaurus

was built like a tank! At 4 m long and weighing a tonne, it didn't have to worry too much about predators. It was covered in hard, bony plates called osteoderms and had a row of spikes down each side.

What they lack in speed, they make up for in clobbering power.

Ankylosaurus was a much later

dinosaur that had a bony club at the end of its tail as well as protective armour of osteoderms.

| PERMIAN 299-251 MYA | TRIASSIC 251-200 MYA | JURASSIC 200-145 MILLION YEARS AGO | CRETACEOUS 145-66 MILLION YEARS AGO | PALEOGENE 66-23 MYA | NEOGENE 23 MYA-NOW |

Similar but Different

Evolution often comes up with similar solutions to the same problems, even thousands of miles – or millions of years – apart. Animals and plants adapt as their needs change. If they need spikes and a thagomizer, they get them!

Stegosaurus

lived in North America. Its thagomizer only had four spikes. But it could still deliver a good thwacking!

Dacentrurus was a

stegosaur from Europe. It went one better than Stegosaurus in swapping some of its plates for spikes. It also had fearsome shoulder spikes –that would stop a predator getting too close.

50

PRECAMBRIAN	CAMBRIAN	ORDOVICIAN	SILURIAN	DEVONIAN	CARBONIFEROUS
4600-542 MYA	542-488 MYA	488-444 MYA	444-416 MYA	416-359 MYA	359-299 MYA

Chialingosaurus lived in China. It has small plates at the front end, which look rather tame. But the back half had a surprise for any hungry predator – a row of sharp spikes down to the end of the tail.

And I thought my teeth were pointy!

Trial and error

When an animal or plant evolves a useful feature – like spikes on a Stegosaur – that organism survives and thrives better than those without the extra help. Over time, the best adapted take over as they are the most successful. If it goes too far – if the spikes get in the way of the Stegosaur's life – they are less successful and Stegosaurs stop getting spikier.

Kentrosaurus

wins! This stegosaur from Tanzania, in Africa, has spikes like massive blades at the end of its tail, plus all the other spikes available!

| PERMIAN 299–251 MYA | TRIASSIC 251–200 MYA | JURASSIC 200–145 MILLION YEARS AGO | CRETACEOUS 145–66 MYA | PALEOGENE 66–23 MYA | NEOGENE 23 MYA–NOW |

51

Fine and Feathery

Dinosaurs were reptiles, so they were scaly, right? Not always! By the Jurassic period, dinosaurs were evolving into all shapes and sizes – there were big ones, small ones, scaly ones and even feathery ones.

Feathers appeared early on in the age of dinosaurs, sometimes on regular dinosaurs and sometimes on animals that were part-way between being dinosaurs and birds. There were probably a lot more feathery dinosaurs than we know about.

Tianyulong

was a little ornithischian dinosaur with filaments (thin strands) like simple feathers. They wouldn't have been any good for flying, but they were a start.

PRECAMBRIAN	CAMBRIAN	ORDOVICIAN	SILURIAN	DEVONIAN	CARBONIFEROUS
4600-542 MYA	542-488 MYA	488-444 MYA	444-416 MYA	416-359 MYA	359-299 MYA

There was a long way to go from filaments to feathers. Filaments might have appeared many times, but only evolved into proper feathers once.

Archaeopteryx

had feathers. About the size of a crow, it flew around Jurassic Germany, flapping or maybe just gliding. But unlike a bird, Archaeopteryx had sharp teeth, claws on its wings and a long, bony tail.

Anchiornis

also had feathers – lots of them! It not only had wings for arms, it also had hind wings, and its feet were covered with feathers, too. Even so, the shape of the wings wasn't well suited to flying and it probably ran along, flapping.

You wouldn't catch me growing feathers.

PERMIAN	TRIASSIC	JURASSIC	CRETACEOUS	PALEOGENE	NEOGENE
299-251 MYA	251-200 MYA	200-145 MILLION YEARS AGO	145-66 MYA	66-23 MYA	23 MYA-NOW

53

New Kids on the Block

Dinosaurs didn't have the Jurassic world to themselves. There were still insects, smaller reptiles, amphibians and the furry descendants of the synapsids. Small at first, often dashing about at night when the dinosaurs were sleeping - the mammals were coming!

Morganucodon was on the way to being a mammal, but was not quite there yet. A small, shrew-like creature, it skittered around the forest floors of Europe, Africa and Asia.

Sinoconodon was another nearly-mammal. It would eat anything it could get – insects, fruit, worms… It wasn't fussy.

Ah, here we go! Now it gets interesting – there's one of my relatives!

PRECAMBRIAN	CAMBRIAN	ORDOVICIAN	SILURIAN	DEVONIAN	CARBONIFEROUS
4600-542 MYA	542-488 MYA	488-444 MYA	444-416 MYA	416-359 MYA	359-299 MYA

Juramaia might be the earliest true mammal. Small, nocturnal and well-adapted to climbing, it was at home and safe in the trees. Like later mammals, Juramaia grew their babies inside their bodies, nourishing them through a **placenta**. After birth, Juramaia mothers produced milk to feed their young.

Fruitafossor was the first mammal to take up digging and to eat only one type of food. It used its strong legs and claws to dig into the ground in search of termites. It had them all to itself – no other mammals learned that trick for 100 million years. Being warm-blooded, mammals control their own body heat and don't need to depend on heat from the sun. Fur helps insulate them too, so they can be active even when it's cold.

Fruitafossor

PERMIAN 299–251 MYA	TRIASSIC 251–200 MYA	JURASSIC 200–145 MILLION YEARS AGO	CRETACEOUS 145–66 MYA	PALEOGENE 66–23 MYA	NEOGENE 23 MYA–NOW

Giants of the Sea

Nothosaurs like Nothosaurus (see page 41) were reptiles that had returned to the rivers. But eventually the reptiles headed right back to the sea where their ancestors started. They developed slowly into the plesiosaurs and came to rule the oceans.

Liopleurodon

Liopleurodon was a giant among sea-reptiles. It could have held a car in its mouth and bitten it in half. In fact, it ate large fish, giant **cephalopods** (like squid), sharks and even dinosaurs. Liopleurodon was a pliosaur – a plesiosaur with a short neck, a large head and larger back flippers than front flippers.

Some of those teeth are bigger than me!

56

| PRECAMBRIAN 4600-542 MYA | CAMBRIAN 542-488 MYA | ORDOVICIAN 488-444 MYA | SILURIAN 444-416 MYA | DEVONIAN 416-359 MYA | CARBONIFEROUS 359-299 MYA |

Leedsichthyus

was an enormous fish with 40,000 teeth – yet it ate only tiny organisms that it filtered through all those teeth. It could grow to 15 m, making it the largest fish ever to live.

Legs and Flippers

Once in the water, reptiles' legs gradually changed to flippers, with lots of short, strong bones packed closely together to make a paddle. A bit like a hand in a mitten!

LEG

FLIPPER

The long neck and small head of

Cryptoclidus

were characteristic of plesiosaurs. Plesiosaurs had lots of tiny teeth, and ate small fish and cephalopods. The opposite of pliosaurs, their front flippers were larger than their back flippers.

| PERMIAN | TRIASSIC | JURASSIC | CRETACEOUS | PALEOGENE | NEOGENE |
| 299-251 MYA | 251-200 MYA | 200-145 MILLION YEARS AGO | 145-66 MYA | 66-23 MYA | 23 MYA-NOW |

57

Some Dark Alleys of Evolution

Evolution comes up with some weird ideas, and they don't always lead anywhere. These adaptations might have suited their owners, but they weren't good enough to make it into the mainstream, or they took useful adaptations just that bit too far.

Therizinosaurus's claws could be a metre long, yet it probably ate plants. They are the largest claws any animal has ever had, and probably got in the way, so growing them any bigger wasn't useful.

	PRECAMBRIAN 4600-542 MYA	CAMBRIAN 542-488 MYA	ORDOVICIAN 488-444 MYA	SILURIAN 444-416 MYA	DEVONIAN 416-359 MYA	CARBONIFEROUS 359-299 MYA

Balaur was

stranded on an island and evolved rather differently from other raptors. Instead of being lean and nimble, Balaur became stocky, with powerful legs that it used to kick its prey.

As for me, I'm small but perfectly formed!

Mamenchisaurus

had the longest neck of any sauropod, at 12 m. It was so long it couldn't lift it high enough to eat from treetops and instead swung it around to hoover up lower-growing plants. So it might as well have had a short neck…

Jeholopterus

was a freaky-looking pterosaur with a short neck and tail, and a snout rather than a beak. It was covered in fine filaments that looked like hair, making it look something like a fierce sugar glider.

Carnotaurus

took the short-arm style of tyrannosaurs to extremes. As it didn't use them, its arms slowly shrank to 50 cm long, making them useless.

PERMIAN
299-251 MYA

TRIASSIC
251-200
MILLION YEARS AGO

JURASSIC
200-145
MILLION YEARS AGO

CRETACEOUS
145-66
MILLION YEARS AGO

PALEOGENE
66-23 MYA

NEOGENE
23 MYA-NOW

59

Looking After Baby

Most reptiles lay their eggs then leave their young to hatch alone. It sounds harsh, but those babies are able to run off and hunt for food immediately, and the adults are safer as they don't have to stay around the nest, a sitting target for predators.

Some dinosaurs did the same: they laid their eggs in a nest, then got on with their own lives.

Orodromeus was one. The babies were well-developed when they hatched, and didn't need parental care. But these eggs and babies were an easy target for predators.

| PRECAMBRIAN 4600-542 MYA | CAMBRIAN 542-488 MYA | ORDOVICIAN 488-444 MYA | SILURIAN 444-416 MYA | DEVONIAN 416-359 MYA | CARBONIFEROUS 359-299 MYA |

Other dinosaurs, like **Maiasaura**, looked after the babies for a while when they hatched, just as many birds do today. Maiasaura lived in herds of up to 10,000 animals. They built nests where the babies hatched and stayed for a while until they grew big enough to find their own food.

When I was little I got milk and cuddles with my mummy. Poor dinosaurs.

An egg outside the body is vulnerable. Plenty of animals eat eggs, and accidents can happen, too. Mammals get around these dangers by growing their babies inside them and giving birth to live young. The young have to be born small, so that they can squeeze out of the mother's body. To help them grow quickly, mammals produce milk from their bodies to nourish their young.

Fighting Machines

The most fearsome dinosaurs had huge, sharp teeth and bone-crushingly powerful jaws. They were the most terrifying predators ever to walk on Earth.

Tyrannosaurus rex

was the most famous theropod of all. It looked perfectly suited to being a fierce predator, but it's possible it spent most of its time scavenging – eating things that had already died or been killed by other dinosaurs. *T. rex*'s jaws delivered the most powerful bite of any creature that has ever lived and it could easily crush bones. Its arms are too small to have been much use for gripping prey – but if it were a scavenger, that wouldn't matter. Tyrannosaurus's teeth were up to 30 cm long – longer than your whole head!

PRECAMBRIAN	CAMBRIAN	ORDOVICIAN	SILURIAN	DEVONIAN	CARBONIFEROUS
4600–542 MYA	542–488 MYA	488–444 MYA	444–416 MYA	416–359 MYA	359–299 MYA

Spinosaurus was the largest theropod ever known, growing to 17 m. Its snout could be up to 1.8 m long (the height of a man) and it had nostrils set well back towards the eyes, which made it well adapted to lurking in shallow water. It's likely that Spinosaurus mostly ate fish, but its powerful back legs meant it could also run fast. You don't need to run fast to catch fish, and it had no predators to fear, so perhaps it also hunted on land.

I don't look like dinner. Lalalalala. You can't see me...

PERMIAN
299-251 MYA

TRIASSIC
251-200 MYA

JURASSIC
200-145 MYA

CRETACEOUS
145-66
MILLION YEARS AGO

PALEOGENE
66-23 MYA

NEOGENE
23 MYA-NOW

63

Don't Worry Your Pretty Head

Triceratops
had horns, which would have been useful in defending itself against an attacking T. rex. But the frill is not for defence. It might have used it to look frightening, like the frill on a chameleon today, or perhaps to look pretty and attract a mate.

Torosaurus

had an even bigger frill – its whole head could be nearly 3 m long!

I feel so plain in comparison!

PRECAMBRIAN	CAMBRIAN	ORDOVICIAN	SILURIAN	DEVONIAN	CARBONIFEROUS
4600–542 MYA	542–488 MYA	488–444 MYA	444–416 MYA	416–359 MYA	359–299 MYA

It's not always clear exactly how a dinosaur's fancy headgear would have been useful. We can watch modern animals, though, and get a clue to some of the possible ways ornate **wattles**, crests, horns and other features might be used.

The thick dome of bone on the head of a

Pachycephalosaurus

might have been used in contests between males to win the best mate. They might have rammed each other in the side with their bony and spiked heads. That wouldn't be lethal, but it would hurt enough to make the point.

Parasaurolophus

has a hollow crest with tubes leading from the nostrils into the skull. It seems likely that the animal could use it to make a trumpeting sound, perhaps to communicate with others, attract a mate, or scare off a rival or predator.

Feathers are the New Scales

Remember the feathery dinosaurs? Well, feathers do lots of useful things so they stuck around. Even some of the most familiar dinosaurs might well have had feathers. Velociraptor probably did – and it seems likely that even T.rex had fluffy down as a baby!

Caudipteryx
looked more bird-like – rather like a pheasant.

Sinosauropteryx
was the first feathered dinosaur ever discovered.

By the cretaceous period, feathers appeared in more than one group: Sinosauropteryx and Caudipteryx were theropods, but Alxasaurus was a therizinosaur and Psittacosaurs was an ornithischian dinosaur.

PRECAMBRIAN	CAMBRIAN	ORDOVICIAN	SILURIAN	DEVONIAN	CARBONIFEROUS
4600-542 MYA	542-488 MYA	488-444 MYA	444-416 MYA	416-359 MYA	359-299 MYA

Being wrapped in feathers is like snuggling in a duvet – it helps to keep you warm. That would have been useful for small dinosaurs that would have got cold quickly. Early dinosaurs were cold-blooded, so they couldn't control their temperature from the inside. On a hot day, they'd be warm and active. On a frosty day, they'd be cold and sluggish – and couldn't run away from predators.

Alxasaurus was a plant-eating dinosaur from Mongolia. Many feathered dinosaurs lived around China and Mongolia.

Psittacosaurus wasn't feathery all over but had a big plume of simple feathers on the tail. They were probably like porcupine quills.

| PERMIAN 299-251 MYA | TRIASSIC 251-200 MYA | JURASSIC 200-145 MYA | CRETACEOUS 145-66 MILLION YEARS AGO | PALEOGENE 66-23 MYA | NEOGENE 23 MYA-NOW |

67

Birds Take Off

So where was evolution going with the feathers and the beaks? You've guessed it – birds! It's not even that dinosaurs evolved into birds. Birds ARE dinosaurs! Dinosaurs are not extinct at all – we are surrounded by them!

Feathers kept dinosaurs warm, and they could have grown them in colourful patterns to attract a mate, or camouflaged patterns to keep them hidden while hunting or being hunted. It's easy to change colour with the seasons by shedding feathers and growing new ones. You can't do that with scales.

Ichthyornis was an early seabird. A bit like a gull, it would dive into the water to pluck out fish to eat. Unlike a gull, it had teeth in its beak! The teeth were only in the middle portion of the beak – the front was toothless, like the beak of a modern bird.

68

PRECAMBRIAN	CAMBRIAN	ORDOVICIAN	SILURIAN	DEVONIAN	CARBONIFEROUS
4600–542 MYA	542–488 MYA	488–444 MYA	444–416 MYA	416–359 MYA	359–299 MYA

Many of the dinosaurs we know now – called avian dinosaurs – use their feathers for flying. The early, non-avian, dinosaurs didn't do that. But as the feathers and muscles developed, they became able to fly and they became birds.

Confuciusornis

was about the size of a crow and lived in China about 125 million years. It was the first bird to have a proper beak without teeth.

Iberomesornis

was no bigger than a modern-day sparrow. It was rather different from a sparrow, though in having a claw on each wing.

Dinosaurs turned into this lot, and I turned into you!

| PERMIAN | TRIASSIC | JURASSIC | CRETACEOUS | PALEOGENE | NEOGENE |
| 299-251 MYA | 251-200 MYA | 200-145 MYA | 145-66 MILLION YEARS AGO | 66-23 MYA | 23 MYA-NOW |

69

Death to the Dinos

Then, 65 million years ago, disaster struck. A terrible catastrophe wiped out the dinosaurs.

Most scientists think a giant **asteroid** or **comet** crashing into Earth just off the coast of Mexico triggered their extinction. The impact would have caused floods, and filled the skies with dust and ash. Plants, starved of sunlight, would have died first. Then the plant-eating animals, and last of all the predators that ate the plant-eaters.

You've got to feel sorry for them! Even the scary ones.

PRECAMBRIAN	CAMBRIAN	ORDOVICIAN	SILURIAN	DEVONIAN	CARBONIFEROUS
4600–542 MYA	542–488 MYA	488–444 MYA	444–416 MYA	416–359 MYA	359–299 MYA

Even before this, the dinosaurs may have been on the way out. Lots of volcanic eruptions were reshaping the land and pouring dust and poisonous gases into the air. Sea levels rose 150 m in less than a million years and the temperature on land might have soared by 10°C. The asteroid or comet could just have been the last straw.

These dramatic changes saw the end of large reptiles, including the plesiosaurs, the pterosaurs and the big dinosaurs – but the birds survived! And the little mammals laid low and waited for the chaos to die down.

Their hour had come!

More Space for Mammals

With the dinosaurs gone, mammals could spread further and grow larger.

That's taking things a bit far.

Starting from tiny insect-eating creatures that looked like shrews, they evolved into all shapes and sizes. Early forms of some modern mammals appeared within a few million years of the death of the dinosaurs.

Andrewsarchus

was like a giant wolf. It was the largest predatory land mammal ever. Its head was more than a metre long.

PRECAMBRIAN 4600-542 MYA	CAMBRIAN 542-488 MYA	ORDOVICIAN 488-444 MYA	SILURIAN 444-416 MYA	DEVONIAN 416-359 MYA	CARBONIFEROUS 359-299 MYA

Carpolestes was the first **primate**-like mammal. It's possibly one of our own very distant ancestors, as humans are a form of primate! It climbed in the trees, eating fruit, seeds and small invertebrates.

Icaronycteris ...ed from insect-eating mammals. An early bat, it had the ...innings of the **echolocation** ...odern bats use to hunt by sound.

It wasn't just the mammals that grew really large. **Titanoboa** was the largest snake ever on land, at 13 m long. It was a metre thick from belly to back! It killed its prey by squeezing it to death with a deadly hug.

PERMIAN
299-251 MYA

TRIASSIC
251-200 MYA

JURASSIC
200-145 MYA

CRETACEOUS
145-66 MYA

PALEOGENE
66-23
MILLION YEARS AGO

NEOGENE
23 MYA-NOW

73

Big Birds

Birds are dinosaurs, and lots of dinosaurs were big, so perhaps it's not surprising that birds began by being very large and scary.

"Terror birds" were fierce, meat-eating birds that lived in South America. The largest, **Brontornis**, stood 3 m tall and weighed 500 kg. It was large and ferocious enough to eat a medium-sized dog at a single gulp!

Brontornis was flightless, with tiny wings, but had massive, powerful legs. South America was an island until 3 million years ago, so life there evolved separately. When South and North America eventually collided, carnivorous mammals competing for food might have driven Brontornis to extinction.

Blimey! When do we small guys get a chance?

74

PRECAMBRIAN
4600-542 MYA

CAMBRIAN
542-488 MYA

ORDOVICIAN
488-444 MYA

SILURIAN
444-416 MYA

DEVONIAN
416-359 MYA

CARBONIFEROUS
359-299 MYA

Gastornis was a less scary flightless bird 2 m tall that stalked the forests of Europe and North America. Its large beak was strong enough to crack coconuts.

Not all Paleogene birds were flightless.

Presbyornis was a bit like a duck, with very long legs and neck. It lived near shallow lakes and filtered water through its beak, eating **crustaceans** and plants.

Argentavis was the largest bird ever. It had a wingspan of 6.4 m. Its wing feathers were the size of Samurai swords! A slightly smaller Argentavis lived in North America until 10,000 years ago, co-existing with humans.

| PERMIAN 299-251 MYA | TRIASSIC 251-200 MYA | JURASSIC 200-145 MYA | CRETACEOUS 145-66 MYA | PALEOGENE 66-23 MILLION YEARS AGO | NEOGENE 23 MYA-NOW |

Works in Water

Do you remember the reptiles that returned to the water and became the plesiosaurs? Some hoofed mammals began to do the same about 50 million years ago, though they kept breathing air. They developed internal ears for sensing vibrations underwater.

Ambulocetus

was a mammal that looked a bit like a crocodile. It lived near India when India was an island. Ambulocetus means "walking whale", but it used its legs as paddles rather than for walking. Ambulocetus might have fed like a crocodile, lurking in the shallows and dragging animals into the water to drown them. It probably swam like an otter, moving its back up and down, with its webbed back feet helping it along. Each toe ended not in a claw but a tiny hoof!

PRECAMBRIAN 4600-542 MYA	CAMBRIAN 542-488 MYA	ORDOVICIAN 488-444 MYA	SILURIAN 444-416 MYA	DEVONIAN 416-359 MYA	CARBONIFEROUS 359-299 MYA

While Ambulocetus was an early whale, **Enaliarctos** was the ancestor of all pinnipeds – sea mammals with flippers, such as seals. It used both front and back flippers to swim, like a modern walrus. Over time, seals evolved from pinnipeds that lost the ability to swim using their front legs, and sea lions from pinnipeds that didn't swim with their back legs. Enaliarctos probably caught its prey in the water and returned to land to eat.

We land mammals need separate fingers. These guys fused theirs into fins!

PERMIAN
299-251 MYA

TRIASSIC
251-200 MYA

JURASSIC
200-145 MYA

CRETACEOUS
145-66 MYA

PALEOGENE
66-23
MILLION YEARS AGO

NEOGENE
23 MYA-NOW

77

Keep on the Grass

The early Paleogene climate was warm, with rainforests even at the poles. But 49 million years ago, the chill returned.

The cause was a simple fern called **Azolla**, which flourished on the surface of the Arctic Ocean at the North Pole. Azolla doubles its mass every 2-3 days, and it bloomed for 800,000 years, drawing carbon dioxide from the air. Carbon dioxide is a greenhouse gas that keeps the world warm. Reducing it was like taking a blanket off the world. Everywhere got colder.

Azolla

There's a nip in the air - it's a good job we mammals have fur!

PRECAMBRIAN	CAMBRIAN	ORDOVICIAN	SILURIAN	DEVONIAN	CARBONIFEROUS
4600-542 MYA	542-488 MYA	488-444 MYA	444-416 MYA	416-359 MYA	359-299 MYA

The colder climate gave grass its chance. It had evolved earlier, but it really took off around 40 million years ago. This meant that animals such as **Paraceratherium**, which fed on leaves from the tropical forests, gradually died out. Paraceratherium is related to modern rhinos, but was eight times the size. It was the largest land mammal ever discovered.

Megacerops was a larger grazer. It was the size of an elephant and looked like a rhino with a forked, Y-shaped horn.

At the same time, great herds of grazing animals took over the new grasslands. One of the smaller grazers was **Mesohippus**, an early horse about the size of a large dog.

| PERMIAN 299-251 MYA | TRIASSIC 251-200 MYA | JURASSIC 200-145 MYA | CRETACEOUS 145-66 MYA | PALEOGENE 66-23 MILLION YEARS AGO | NEOGENE 23 MYA-NOW |

Chapter 6: The Start of Now

New World Order

The modern world has taken shape over the last 23 million years. Mountain ranges such as the Alps, Himalayas and Pyrenees grew up, South America joined onto North America, and India joined onto Asia.

Now animals could migrate between North and South America. Snakes, cats, deer, tapirs and wolves moved south, and possums, armadillos, sloths and hummingbirds moved north. Then each adapted to their new homes.

As the world got colder, conifer forests grew in the north, then broad-leafed forests and dry grasslands emerged further south.

Ah, I can relate to that little guy!

PRECAMBRIAN	CAMBRIAN	ORDOVICIAN	SILURIAN	DEVONIAN	CARBONIFEROUS
4600–542 MYA	542–488 MYA	488–444 MYA	444–416 MYA	416–359 MYA	359–299 MYA

Chalicotherium

looked like a cross between a horse and a sloth and walked on its hind feet and its front knuckles. It had long, curved claws, which would have been in the way or worn down if it walked without holding them back. Although they looked fierce, Chalicotherium used them for raking or pulling on plants.

The odd-looking **Ceratogaulus** was a horned gopher with long, sharp claws. It used the claws for digging, but we don't know what the horns were for - perhaps to scare away predators, as they'd make it a spiky mouthful.

| PERMIAN | TRIASSIC | JURASSIC | CRETACEOUS | PALEOGENE | NEOGENE |
| 299-251 MYA | 251-200 MYA | 200-145 MYA | 145-66 MYA | 66-23 MYA | 23 MILLION YEARS AGO - NOW |

81

Nearly Human

Around 7 million years ago, one group of primates evolved into chimpanzees and another into humans.

You guys should have kept a grasping toe. It's useful!

Homo ergaster
– lived 1.5 million years ago.
– was tall and slender.
– had little body hair.

Australopithecus
– was chimp-sized but had a bigger brain.
– walked on two feet .
– lived all over Africa.

Homo habilis
– was the first human species.
– used stone tools, so they could prepare food that needed less chewing.
– less chewing meant their cheek muscles shrank to look like ours.

Ardipithecus
– lived 4 or 5 million years ago.
– had smaller brains than us.
– still had an ape-like grasping toe for climbing trees.

PRECAMBRIAN	CAMBRIAN	ORDOVICIAN	SILURIAN	DEVONIAN	CARBONIF
4600-542 MYA	542-488 MYA	488-444 MYA	444-416 MYA	416-359 MYA	359-29

Homo heidelbergensis

- was the first human species in Europe.
- made advanced tools of wood and stone.
- might have used language.

Homo neanderthalensis

- evolved around 200,000 years ago.
- lived alongside modern humans until 30,000 years ago.

Homo erectus

- looked a lot like us.
- moved out of Africa into Asia.
- may have survived until 100,000 years ago.

Homo sapiens

Us!

Fierce Foes

Our early ancestors faced alternating icy and warm periods over the last 900,000 years. But not only was it really cold a lot of the time - there were also some giant, fierce predators.

Arctodus was one of the largest land-based carnivores of all time. Although a 4 m long bear is a pretty scary idea, Arctodus probably mostly ate animals that something else had killed. Early human hunters might have been more of a threat to Arctodus than it was to them.

PRECAMBRIAN	CAMBRIAN	ORDOVICIAN	SILURIAN	DEVONIAN	CARBONIFEROUS
4600-542 MYA	542-488 MYA	488-444 MYA	444-416 MYA	416-359 MYA	359-299 MYA

Smilodon was a ferocious, sabre-toothed cat - probably the largest cat ever. Smilodons were more heavily built than lions and tigers, and hunted large plant-eaters such as bison and camels. They had massive canine teeth, up to 28 cm long!

Megalodon was a bit like a great white shark, but weighed ten times as much as *T. rex* and was 18 m long. It had teeth bigger than your hand and jaws large enough for an adult human to stand upright in (though that wouldn't be a smart thing to do).

Megalodon

Do you like to be beside the seaside? You might not if Megalodon were around!

PERMIAN 299-251 MYA	TRIASSIC 251-200 MYA	JURASSIC 200-145 MYA	CRETACEOUS 145-66 MYA	PALEOGENE 66-23 MYA	NEOGENE 23 MILLION YEARS AGO - NOW

Super-sloths and Mega-mammoths

Being large helps mammals keep warm. When the last ice age began, about 2.5 million years ago, huge mammals were well adapted to the climate and flourished. But when the weather warmed up, the super-sized versions died out.

Woolly mammoths

were the last type of mammoths to evolve. Their huge size, warm, woolly coat and a layer of special fat up to 10 cm thick kept them warm in the snow.

PRECAMBRIAN 4600–542 MYA	CAMBRIAN 542–488 MYA	ORDOVICIAN 488–444 MYA	SILURIAN 444–416 MYA	DEVONIAN 416–359 MYA	CARBONIFEROUS 359–299 MYA

It's not just elephants that came in a furry variety. **Elasmotherium** was a hairy rhino with a giant horn used for fighting, showing off and sweeping snow from the grass it wanted to eat.

The giant ground-sloth **Megatherium** was as big as a modern elephant. It ambled around forests and grasslands, pulling down branches with its hooked claws.

Glyptodon was related to Megatherium and to modern sloths and armadillos. It had thick plates of bone making an armoured dome over its back, and was the size and shape of a Volkswagen Beetle.

PERMIAN	TRIASSIC	JURASSIC	CRETACEOUS	PALEOGENE	NEOGENE
299-251 MYA	251-200 MYA	200-145 MYA	145-66 MYA	66-23 MYA	23 MILLION YEARS AGO -NOW

Oops, Near Miss

Seventy-four thousand years ago, a catastrophic eruption of the super-volcano Toba in Indonesia might have brought humans to the brink of extinction.

Samosir Island

THE TOBA VOLCANO

Lake Toba

Lake Toba is formed of the four caldera (mouths) of the Toba super-volcano. Samosir Island is made of solidified lava from its last, gigantic eruption.

It was the largest eruption of the last two million years, and caused a "volcanic winter'" blocking the sunlight and sending temperatures plunging. A layer of volcanic ash 15 cm deep covered South East Asia, and poisonous gases poured into the sky. Plants and animals died, starving early humans until only a few thousand survived.

This sort of thing is becoming a habit!

PRECAMBRIAN 4600-542 MYA	CAMBRIAN 542-488 MYA	ORDOVICIAN 488-444 MYA	SILURIAN 444-416 MYA	DEVONIAN 416-359 MYA	CARBONIFEROUS 359-299 MYA

The huge variety in modern humans – in skin colour, hair colour, size and shape - has come about over the last 70,000 years. This is just what would happen if the human race had expanded quickly from a fairly small number of people who spread widely over the Earth. When a population shrinks and then expands again from a small number of individuals it's called a "bottleneck" in evolution.

Soon after Toba, humans migrated out of Africa to spread all around the world.

Homo sapiens could use tools, fire and language. By hunting and then farming, they affected the evolution of other animals and plants. They took over from *Homo neanderthalensis* and became the only human species. They became us.

| PERMIAN 299-251 MYA | TRIASSIC 251-200 MYA | JURASSIC 200-145 MYA | CRETACEOUS 145-66 MYA | PALEOGENE 66-23 MYA | NEOGENE 23 MILLION YEARS AGO - NOW |

89

Evolution is Still Going

Animals and plants are always evolving. Organisms that can adapt succeed, and others die out. That's evolution. But humans are moving the goalposts. Our impact on the natural world has been immense, greater than the impact of any previous animal.

The **Moa** was a giant bird that lived in New Zealand until it was hunted to extinction in the 1500s. Another flightless bird, the **Dodo**, died out after people destroyed its habitat and brought in animals that ate it. The **Baiji river dolphin** was last seen in 2006. The river it lived in had become polluted and over-used.

Moa

Dodo

Baiji River Dolphin

| PRECAMBRIAN 4600-542 MYA | CAMBRIAN 542-488 MYA | ORDOVICIAN 488-444 MYA | SILURIAN 444-416 MYA | DEVONIAN 416-359 MYA | CARBONIFEROUS 359-299 MYA |

The story is not always bad.
Przewalski's horse
was extinct in the wild, but
has been bred in zoos and
released into Mongolia,
where it once lived.

Crow

Przewalski's horse

Animals are adapting all the time.
Crows in Japan have learned to drop
nuts on roads so that cars crack them
open! More worryingly, bacteria and
viruses evolve quickly, so that some
medicines no longer work.

We are still evolving too. Maybe we will be
the first species to spread to other planets.
Maybe we will take charge of our own
evolution, with **genetic engineering**. Maybe
humans will even be as successful as the
dinosaurs and last another 165 million years.

What will I
be next...?

PERMIAN	TRIASSIC	JURASSIC	CRETACEOUS	PALEOGENE	NEOGENE
299-251 MYA	251-200 MYA	200-145 MYA	145-66 MYA	66-23 MYA	23 MILLION YEARS AGO - NOW

Glossary

Amphibian: cold-blooded vertebrate that lives both in water and on land. Amphibians lay eggs in the water that hatch into a juvenile stage – such as tadpoles – that later change into the adult form.

Arthropod: animal with a segmented body and at least six jointed legs. Arthropods have a hard outer shell. Insects, crabs and centipedes are all examples of arthropods.

Asteroid: large lump of rock and metal that travels through outer space.

Atmosphere: the blanket of gases surrounding a planet. Earth's atmosphere is made up of various gases, mostly nitrogen and oxygen.

Carbon dioxide: gas made of carbon and oxygen. Plants take carbon dioxide from the atmosphere and replace it with oxygen.

Carnivore: animal that eats meat (other animals).

Cells: tiny component of living things. Single-celled organisms have only one cell. Multi-cellular organisms have cells of different types that carry out different tasks.

Cephalopod: type of mollusc that lives in sea water, including squid and octopus. Cephalopods are soft-bodied animals with a head and tentacles.

Cold-blooded: unable to control body temperature independently. Cold-blooded animals are active when the environment is hot, and slow when it is cold.

Comet: found in space. Chunk of ice and rock dust. When a comet is close to the sun, it has a glowing tail of gas.

Domination: rule or control.

Echolocation: method of perception used by bats, dolphins, whales and some other animals that works by measuring the time it takes for a sound to bounce back as an echo.

Herbivore: animal that eats only plants.

Gait: style of walking, determined by the position and shape of the legs, feet and hips.

Gene: unit of information about inherited characteristics. The genes of an organism carry a code that describes every feature of it. Genes are the means of passing characteristics such as size and colour from parents to offspring.

Genetic engineering: changing the genes of an organism to alter its characteristics.

Gills: organs used by animals that live in water to take oxygen from the water. They perform the same task as lungs perform in land-based animals.

Mammal: vertebrate animal that has body fur or hair of some type. Most mammals grow their young inside their bodies and produce milk for them after they are born.

Mass extinction: widespread destruction of many species of plants and animals over a relatively short period of time.

Microbe: tiny living organism, so small it they can only be seen through a microscope.

Mollusc: soft-bodied animal, with or without a shell.

Nucleus: centre of a cell, containing the genetic organism's material and structures important in the working of the cell.

Nutritious: containing the nutrients an animal needs to grow and stay healthy.

Omnivore: animal that eats both plants and animals.

Ornithischian: type of plant-eating dinosaur with a hard beak. Parasaurolophus is an example of an ornithischian dinosaur.

Pangaea: a supercontinent that formed 300 million years ago.

Placenta: internal organ grown by a pregnant female mammal to nourish the unborn baby.

Primate: mammal that has hands and feet capable of grasping, a large brain and well-developed vision. Humans, monkey and lemurs are examples of primates.

Proboscis: in vertebrates, an extra-long nose, such as an elephant's trunk. In insects, it is a tube that forms part of the mouth

Reproduce: create offspring (more organisms of the same type).

Reptile: cold-blooded vertebrate that lays eggs. Reptiles have scaly skin.

Sauropod: type of large dinosaur that walked on all four legs, ate plants, and had a long neck and long tail. Diplodocus is an example of a sauropod.

Species: distinct category of organisms. A species is distinguished by its genes; organisms usually only reproduce with members of their own species.

Sperm: male reproductive cell. A sperm (produced by male animals) combines with an egg cell (produced by female animals) in the process of reproduction.

Swim bladder: organ which allows a fish to control the depth at which it swims. The swim bladder fills with gas and acts as a float.

Tetrapod: vertebrate with four limbs. Reptiles, amphibians, mammals and birds are tetrapods.

Theropod: type of dinosaur that walked on two strong back legs. Most theropods were carnivorous. *T. rex* is an example of a theropod.

Vertebrate: animal with a backbone.

Warm-blooded: able to control body temperature independently. Warm-blooded animals can make their own body heat, and have fur to help keep them warm.

Wattles are pieces of skin that sit on the top of the head or neck of many animals – think of the neck of a turkey!

Index

Picture credits

See you in a few more million years...